OXFORD

# R. VAUGHAN WILLIAMS

# SYMPHONY NO. 5

# IN D MAJOR

EDITED BY
PETER HORTON

STUDY SCORE

# R. VAUGHAN WILLIAMS

# SYMPHONY NO. 5
## IN D MAJOR

EDITED BY
PETER HORTON

STUDY SCORE

MUSIC DEPARTMENT

OXFORD
UNIVERSITY PRESS

# OXFORD
### UNIVERSITY PRESS

Great Clarendon Street, Oxford OX2 6DP, England
198 Madison Avenue, New York, NY 10016, USA

Oxford University Press is a department of the University of Oxford.
It furthers the University's aim of excellence in research, scholarship,
and education by publishing worldwide

Oxford is a registered trade mark of Oxford University Press
in the UK and in certain other countries

First published 2008
First published in paperback 2009

1  3  5  7  9  10  8  6  4  2

ISBN  978–0–19–336824–8

Music origination by Barnes Music Engraving Ltd., East Sussex
Printed in Great Britain on acid-free paper by
Halstan & Co. Ltd., Amersham, Bucks

# CONTENTS

# PREFACE

The Fifth Symphony, completed in 1943 in the midst of the Second World War, marks the climax of the modal-lyrical aspect of Vaughan Williams's music, reaching back to the *Fantasia on a Theme by Thomas Tallis* of 1910, *Flos Campi* of 1925, and *Job* of 1930, to name only the most prominent works in this style. None of the four subsequent symphonies revisited this style to anything like the same degree. Although emphatically not a programme-symphony, it is also closely linked with Bunyan's *The Pilgrim's Progress*, dramatization of which obsessed Vaughan Williams from 1906, when he wrote incidental music for an amateur production, to the full-scale opera (or Morality as he called it) first performed at Covent Garden in 1951 and on which he had worked intermittently since completing the one-act episode *The Shepherds of the Delectable Mountains* in 1921.

He seems to have begun sketching the symphony around 1938, using several themes composed for the opera, which he had apparently given up hope of finishing. He tried out some of these ideas in two items of music for military band which he contributed to a pageant called *England's Pleasant Land* at Milton Court, Westcott, Surrey, on 9 July 1938. 'Exit of the Ghosts of the Past' contains much of the subsidiary material of the symphony's first movement, Preludio, and the chorale-like melody for horns in the Scherzo, while 'Funeral March for the Old Order' opens with the principal material of the Preludio in a different key, and there are other links to the symphony.

A list of the material shared between the opera and the symphony may be found in *A Catalogue of the Works of Ralph Vaughan Williams* (Oxford University Press, 2nd edn. 1996). It occurs in the first, third, and fourth movements but the treatment is different. The most obvious dramatic quotation occurs at the beginning of the Romanza when the cor anglais has the theme which in the opera (act 1, scene 2) is sung to the words 'He hath given me rest by his sorrow and life by his death'. Vaughan Williams originally inscribed these words above the symphony movement but deleted them before publication. He also changed the dedication from 'Dedicated (without permission and with sincerest flattery) to Jean Sibelius, whose great example is worthy of all imitation' to 'Dedicated without permission to Jean Sibelius'.

In February 1943 Vaughan Williams offered the symphony to Sir Henry J. Wood for the Promenade Concerts that summer. 'Though not technically difficult', he wrote, '[it] will I imagine want a good deal of rehearsal to make it "come off"' (he revised points of detail in 1951). In the event Wood was ill and VW conducted it himself on 24 June in the Royal Albert Hall. He wrote to Wood: 'The orchestra [London Philharmonic] were splendid – and as I made no serious mistakes we had a very fine performance.' (Apart from *A Sea Symphony* in 1910 it was the only one of his symphonies of which he conducted the first performance.) To many listeners it came as a vision of peace during the dark days of the war. Others thought it was the 70-year-old composer's Nunc Dimittis, a benevolent farewell. But though words like 'serenity' and 'radiance' are inescapable when discussing the symphony, we can hear today that this music is not all benediction and serenity, and that at one point it was associated in his mind not only with Bunyan's pilgrim but, more darkly, with ghosts of the past and a funeral march for the old order.

MICHAEL KENNEDY
August 2007

For a full description of the editorial method employed in this score, together with a critical commentary, please see the cloth-bound edition, ISBN 978–0–19–335942–0.

# SYMPHONY NO. 5

## IN D MAJOR

# ORCHESTRATION

Piccolo (doubling Flute 2)
2 Flutes
Oboe
Cor Anglais
2 Clarinets
2 Bassoons
2 Horns
2 Trumpets
2 Tenor Trombones
Bass Trombone
Timpani
Strings

Duration: *c.*35 minutes

*Dedicated without permission to Jean Sibelius*

# Symphony No. 5 in D major

R. VAUGHAN WILLIAMS

## 1. Preludio

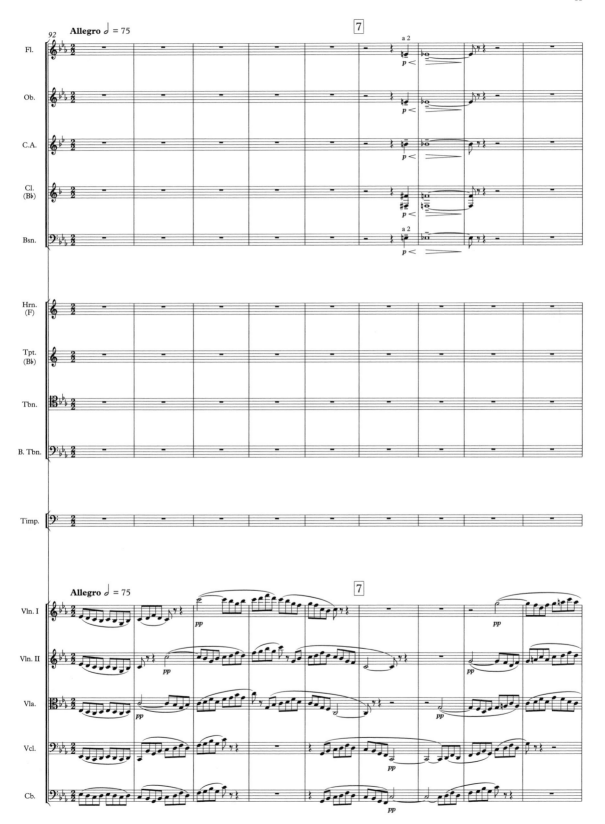

# 2. Scherzo

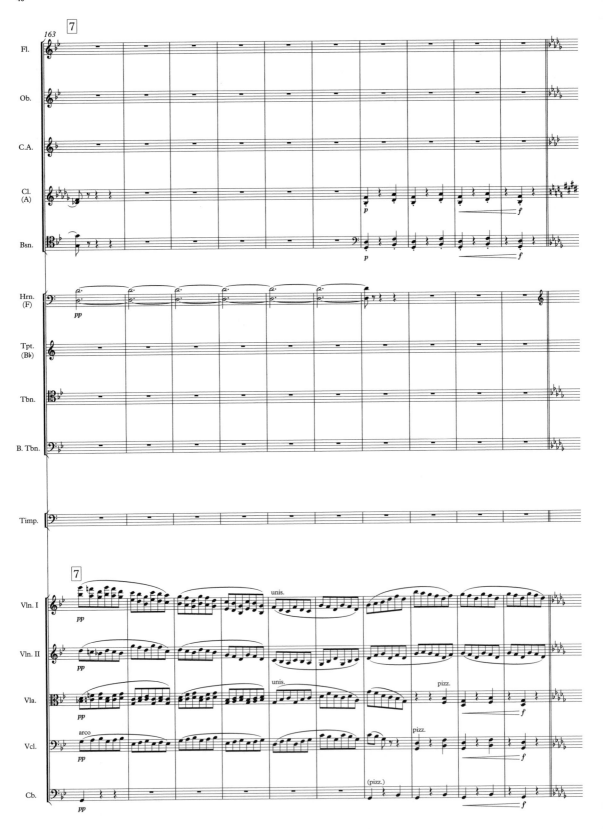

43

11
238
Fl. 1 2
Ob.
C.A.
Cl. (A)
Bsn.
Hrn. (F)
Tpt. (B♭)
Tbn.
B. Tbn.
Timp.
tr
Vln. I
Vln. II
Vla.
Vcl.
Cb.
pizz.
(pizz.)
arco
pp
f
p

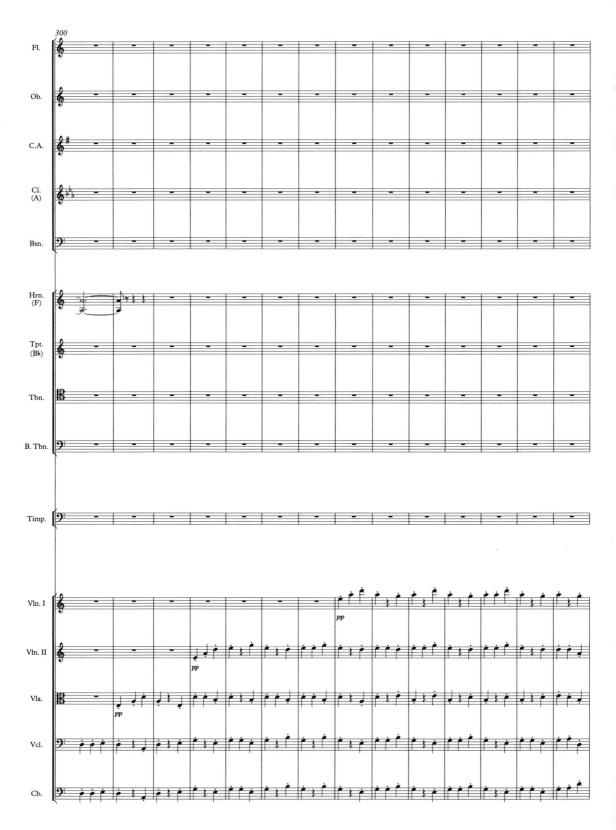

55

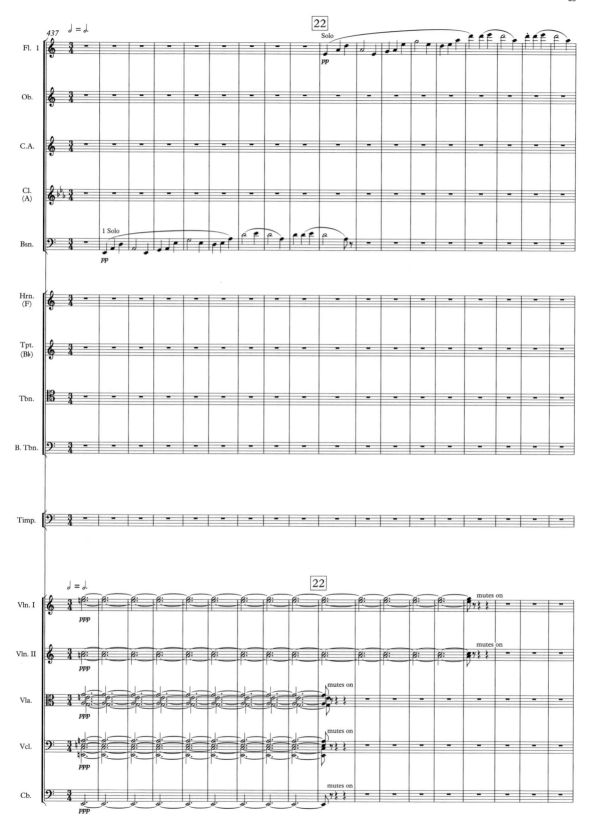

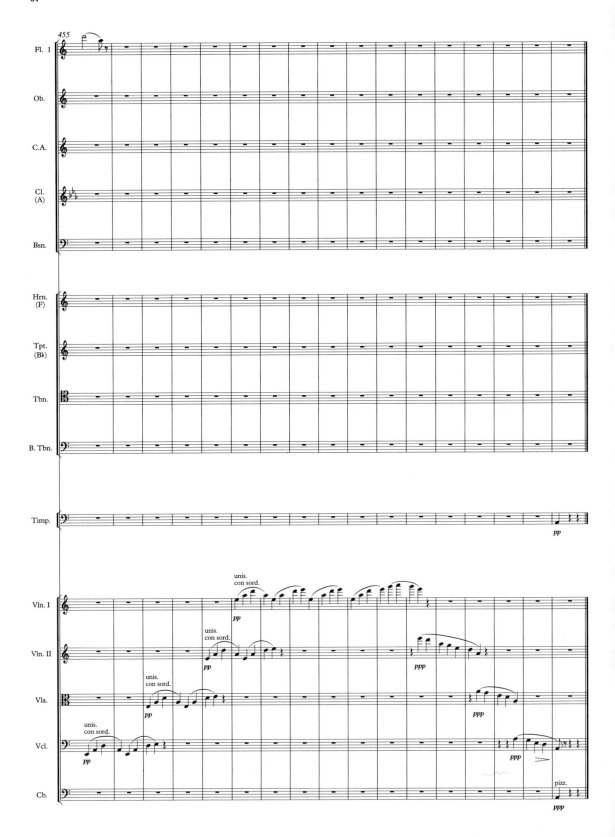

# 3. Romanza

72

**9 Pochino più movimento**

# 4. Passacaglia

104

# OXFORD
UNIVERSITY PRESS

www.oup.com

ISBN 978-0-19-336824-8

9 780193 368248